Bush Theatre 50
EST. 1972

A Bush Theatre Production

AUGUST IN ENGLAND

by Lenny Henry

T0323177

Opened on 28 April 2023
Bush Theatre, London

AUGUST IN ENGLAND

by Lenny Henry

Cast and Creative Team

Writer & Performer	Lenny Henry
Co-Directors	Daniel Bailey & Lynette Linton
Set & Costume Designer	Natalie Pryce
Lighting Designer	Jai Morjaria
Sound Designer & Composer	Duramaney Kamara
Video Designer	Gino Ricardo Green
Movement Director	Shelley Maxwell
Voice & Dialect Coach	Hazel Holder
Dramaturg	Deirdre O'Halloran
Windrush Consultant	Amelia Gentleman
Costume Supervisor	Malena Arcucci
Production Manager	Pete Rickards for eStage
Assistant Production Manager	Lewis Champney for eStage
Company Stage Manager	Chloe Wilson
Assistant Stage Manager	Sophie Haliburn

With special thanks to Michael Braithwaite, Gloria Fletcher and Judy Griffith.

Cast and Creative Team

LENNY HENRY | WRITER & PERFORMER

Lenny Henry has risen from being a cult star on children's television to becoming one of Britain's best-known comedians, as well as a writer, philanthropist and award-winning actor.

In recent years Lenny has starred in *The Comedy of Errors* (National); *Fences* (Duchess); *The Resistable Rise of Arturo Ui* (Donmar Warehouse) and most recently August Wilson's *King Hedley II* (Theatre Royal Stratford East).

Lenny's television credits include *Broadchurch*, *The Syndicate*, *The Long Song* and his biographic *Danny and the Human Zoo*. Lenny's production company, Douglas Road, has achieved success in partnership with Burning Bright on the recently acclaimed *The Commonwealth Kid* documentary and has a host of other programmes in the pipeline.

As a co-founder of Comic Relief Lenny was delighted to announce this year that the British public has donated over £1 billion to Comic Relief over the last 30 years.

Lenny is a strong advocate for diversity, taking his work on the subject to Cannes in order to deliver the Keynote speech launching the idea of offering tax breaks for diversity, as well as talks given in Rome to the global TV and film insider audience.

Lenny was chosen by Baroness Doreen Lawrence to interview three beneficiaries of the Stephen Lawrence trust at his memorial in 2018.

Lenny recently released his memoir, *Who Am I Again?*, in October 2019.

He has been a Trustee of the National Theatre since February 2016.

DANIEL BAILEY | CO-DIRECTOR

Daniel Bailey is Associate Artistic Director of the Bush Theatre. He was previously Associate Director at Birmingham Repertory Theatre, originally joining The REP as part of the Regional Theatre Young Director Scheme where his work included artist development programmes for writers, theatre-makers and directors. He has previously been Resident Director at the National Theatre Studio, Associate Artist at Theatre Royal Stratford East and Resident Assistant Director at The Finborough Theatre. Daniel studied Modern Drama at Brunel University before participating in the Young Vic's Introduction to Directing.

Theatre directing credits include: *Red Pitch* and *The High Table* (Bush); *Blue/Orange*, *Concubine*, *Stuff*, *I Knew You*, *Abuelo*, *Jump! We'll Catch You*, *Made In India/Britain* and *Exhale* (Birmingham Repertory Theatre); *Unknown Rivers* (Hampstead); *Covered* (New Heritage Theatre).

Film director credits include: *Can I Live?* (Complicité); *On Belonging* (Young Vic); *Malachi, Y.O.L.O. Therapy* (S.E.D); *Floating On Clouds* (Kingdom Entertainment Group).

LYNETTE LINTON | CO-DIRECTOR

Lynette Linton has been Artistic Director of the Bush Theatre since 2019. Her first season was a series of ground-breaking debuts from UK and Irish writers. She was previously Resident Assistant Director at the Donmar Warehouse and Associate Director at the Gate Theatre.

Lynette directed the UK premiere of Lynn Nottage's Pulitzer Prize-winning play *Sweat* (Donmar Warehouse, Gielgud Theatre) for which she won 'Best Director' at the inaugural Black British Theatre awards. *Sweat* also won the Evening Standard award for 'Best Play' and was nominated for an Oliver award for 'Best New Play'.

Her production of *Richard II* (Shakespeare's Globe) which she directed with Adjoa Andoh, marked the first ever company of women of colour in a Shakespeare play on a major UK stage. Lynette recently made her National Theatre debut directing a new production of American writer Pearl Cleage's *Blues for an Alabama Sky*.

Additional directing credits include: Beru Tessema's *House of Ife* and Jackie Kay's *Chiaroscuro* (both Bush); *Assata Taught Me* (Gate); *Function* (National Youth Theatre); *This Is* (ArtsEd); *Naked* (VAULT Festival); *This Wide Night* (Albany). She was also co-director on *Chicken Palace* (Stratford East). TV credits include: *My Name is Leon* (BBC), for which she has been nominated for a BAFTA.

Theatre writing credits include: *Hashtag Lightie* (Arcola); *Chicken Palace* and *Step* (Stratford East). TV writing credits include: *Look at Me* (ITV).

She is co-founder of theatre and film production company Black Apron Entertainment who produced *Passages: A Windrush Celebration* with the Royal Court, a project she also curated.

NATALIE PRYCE | SET & COSTUME DESIGNER

Natalie Pryce's set and costume design credits include: *Sunny Side Up* (Theatre Peckham); *Of the Cut, Me for the World* (Young Vic); *The Gift, Red Velvet* (RADA); *846 Live* at (Stratford East); *Ducklings* (Royal Exchange). She was Co-Set and Costume Designer for: *For All the Women Who Thought They Were Mad* (Hackney Showroom); *Not Now, Bernard* (Unicorn).

Theatre Costume Design credits include: *Newsies* (Troubadour Wembley Park Theatre); *Hamlet* (Bristol Old Vic); *Playboy of the West Indies* (Birmingham Rep); *A Number* (Old Vic); *Old Bridge* (Bush); *White Noise* (Bridge); *Is God Is* (Royal Court); *Anna X* (West End); *Tales of the Turntable* (Zoonation); and Costume Supervisor for *The Winter's Tale* (Shakespeare's Globe). Film credits include: *Good Grief, Swept Under Rug* and *My Name is Leon* (as Costume Trainee) .

Natalie won the Black British Theatre Award Winner for Costume Design Recognition in 2020.

JAI MORJARIA | LIGHTING DESIGNER

Jai Morjaria trained at RADA and won the 2016 Association of Lighting Designer's ETC Award.

Design credits include: *Othello* (National); *Graceland* (Royal Court); *The Trials* (Donmar Warehouse); *Accidental Death of an Anarchist* (Lyric Hammersmith/ Sheffield Theatres); *Wuthering Heights* (St Ann's Warehouse/National/US tour/Wise Children); *My Son's a Queer (But What Can You Do?)* (Ambassadors/Garrick/Underbelly/Turbine); *Chasing Hares* (Young Vic); *Cruise* (Duchess); *The Cherry Orchard* (Yard/HOME); *Cherry Jezebel* (Liverpool Everyman); *House of Ife*, *Lava* (Bush); *Worth* (Arcola/New Earth); *Birthmarked* (Bristol Old Vic); *Big Big Sky*, *The Hoes* (Hampstead); *The Sorcerer's Apprentice* (Northern Stage); *Out of the Dark* (Rose Theatre Kingston); *Shuck'n'Jive*, *Whitewash* (Soho); *Anansi the Spider* (Unicorn); *I'll Take You to Mrs. Cole* (Complicité); *Glory* (Duke's/Red Ladder); *Cuzco* (Theatre503); *Losing Venice* (Orange Tree); *Out There on Fried Meat Ridge Road* (White Bear/Trafalgar Studios 2).

DURAMANEY KAMARA | SOUND DESIGNER & COMPOSER

Duramaney Kamara was the composer, sound designer and resident DJ for Dismantle, a festival of work by Project 2036 at the Bush Theatre.

Composer and sound designer credits include: *House of Ife* (Bush); *Sucker Punch* (Queen's Theatre, Hornchurch); *Bootycandy* (Gate); *Anansi the Spider* (Unicorn); *Bangers* (Soho).

Theatre performance credits include: *Boy* (Almeida); *The Response* (Seagull/Mercury). Film performance credits include: *Yardie*, *What Happened to Evie*.

GINO RICARDO GREEN | VIDEO DESIGNER

Gino Ricardo Green is a director and video/projection designer. He is co-founder of Black Apron Entertainment.

Credits as Video/Projection Designer include: *Othello* (National, Co-Video Designer); *The Ballad of St Johns Carpark* (Icon); *Treason: The Musical in Concert* (West End); *That is Not Who I Am* (Royal Court); *Kabul Goes Pop: Music Television Afghanistan* (Brixton House & Hightide); *Edge* (NYT); *Lava* (Bush); *Children's Children* (Director of Photography/Editor – English Touring Theatre); *Beyond the Canon*, *Poor Connection* (RADA); *Sweat* (Donmar Warehouse/West End); *Passages: A Windrush Celebration* (Black Apron at the Royal Court); *Hashtag Lightie* (Arcola); *Lightie* (Projection Designer – Gate).

Credits as Associate Video/Projection Designer include: *Small Island* (National); *Get Up, Stand Up! The Bob Marley Musical* (West End); *Be More Chill* (The Other Palace/West End).

SHELLEY MAXWELL | MOVEMENT DIRECTOR

Shelley Maxwell's credits include: *The Secret Life of Bees* (Almeida); *Best of Enemies* (Noël Coward/Young Vic); *Tartuffe* (Birmingham Repertory Theatre); *The Time Traveller's Wife: The Musical* (Storyhouse); *Get Up, Stand Up! The Bob Marley Story*, *Cinderella* (Lyric); *J'Ouvert* (Harold Pinter/Theatre503); *After Life*, *'Master Harold'...and the boys*, *Hansard*, *Antony and Cleopatra*, *Twelfth Night* (National); *Nine Night* (National/Trafalgar Studios); *Equus* (Stratford East/Trafalgar Studios);*Tartuffe* (RSC); *Macbeth* (Shakespeare's Globe); *Faustus* (Headlong at Lyric & Birmingham Repertory Theatre); *Grey* (Ovalhouse); *King Hedley II* (Stratford East); *Cougar*, *Dealing with Clair* (Orange Tree); *Winter*, *Why It's Kicking off Everywhere* (Young Vic); *Cuttin' It* (Young Vic & Royal Court); *A Streetcar Named Desire* (Nuffield, Clwyd Theatr Cymru & English Touring Theatre); *Rules for Living* (Royal & Derngate, the Rose Kingston & English Touring Theatre); *Apologia* (English Theatre Frankfurt). Television includes: *Anansi Boys* (upcoming on Amazon).

Shelley won the award for Best Choreographer at the inaugural Black British Theatre Awards in 2019 for her work on *Equus*.

HAZEL HOLDER | VOICE & DIALECT COACH

Hazel Holder's theatre credits include: *Blues for an Alabama Sky*, *Rockets and Blue Lights*, *Death of England: Delroy*, *Death of England*, *Small Island*, *Nine Night*, *Barber Shop Chronicles*, *Angels in America*, *Les Blancs*, *Ma Rainey's Black Bottom* (National); *Best of Enemies*, *Cock*, *To Kill a Mockingbird*, *Get Up, Stand Up! The Bob Marley Story*, *The Glass Menagerie*, *Constellations*, *2:22*, *Tina: The Tina Turner Musical*, *Dreamgirls* (West End); *Seven Methods of Killing Kylie Jenner*, *ear for eye* (Royal Court); *Mandela*, *Fairview*, *Death of a Salesman*, *The Convert* (Young Vic); *The Doll's House Part II*, *Marys Seacole*, *Love and Other Acts of Violence* (Donmar Warehouse); *Jitney* (Old Vic); *Retrograde*, *The Wife of Willesden*, *Pass Over* (Kiln); *Richard II* (Sam Wanamaker Playhouse); *Guys and Dolls* (Talawa); *Caroline, or Change* (Chichester, Hampstead, West End); *Eclipsed* (Gate); *A Midsummer Night's Dream* (Shakespeare North).

Film credits include: *Drift*, *Aisha* (for Letitia Wright), *The Silent Twins*. TV credits include: *The Power*, *Mood*, *The Baby*, *Small Axe*.

DEIRDRE O'HALLORAN | DRAMATURG

Deirdre O'Halloran is the Literary Manager at the Bush Theatre, working to identify and build relationships with new writers, commission new work and guide plays to the stage.

At the Bush she's dramaturged plays including the Olivier award-winning *Baby Reindeer* by Richard Gadd and *The P Word* by Waleed Akhtar. Other plays at the Bush include *Lava* by Benedict Lombe, *An Adventure* by Vinay Patel, *Paradise Now!* by Margaret Perry and *Red Pitch* by Tyrell Williams.

Deirdre was previously Literary Associate at Soho Theatre, where she worked as a dramaturg on plays including *Girls* by Theresa Ikoko and *Fury* by Phoebe Eclair-Powell. She led on Soho Theatre's Writers' Lab programme and the biennial Verity Bargate Award. As a freelancer, Deirdre has also been a reader for Out of Joint, Sonia Friedman Productions and Papatango.

AMELIA GENTLEMAN | WINDRUSH CONSULTANT

Amelia Gentleman is a British journalist. She is a reporter for the Guardian and author of *The Windrush Betrayal, Exposing the Hostile Environment*. She won the Paul Foot award, Cudlipp award, an Amnesty award, journalist of the year British journalism awards and London press club print journalist of the year for Windrush investigations. She has also won the Orwell prize, feature and specialist writer of the year. Previously she reported from Delhi, Paris and Moscow.

MALENA ARCUCCI | COSTUME SUPERVISOR

Malena Arcucci is a theatre designer and costume supervisor, born and raised in Buenos Aires and based in London. She is co-artistic director of Mariana Malena Theatre Company.

Design credits include: *Strangers Like Me* (NT Connect & Hackney Shed); *The Bit Players* (Southwark); *Friday Night Love Poem* (Zoo, Edinburgh); *Point of No Return* (Actor's Centre); *La Llorona* (Dance City Newcastle);*The Two of Us* (Theatre Deli); *Playing Latinx* (Camden People's Theatre); and various productions in Buenos Aires, Argentina. Her credits as Associate Designer include: *Dear Elizabeth* (Gate); *Chiaroscuro* (Bush); *Thebes Land, Tamburlaine* (Arcola).

Costume Supervisor credits include: *Sucker Punch* (Queen's Theatre, Hornchurch); Bootycandy (Gate); *Super High Resolution* (Soho); *The Boys are Kissing, Milk and Gall, Moreno* (Theatre503); *Blues for an Alabama Sky* (National, as Assistant); *The Cherry Orchard* (Yard/HOME); *Chasing Hares* (Young Vic); *House of Ife* (Bush); *Lotus Beauty, Raya* (Hampstead).

PETE RICKARDS FOR ESTAGE | PRODUCTION MANAGER

Pete Rickards is an experienced Production Manager and Technical Consultant within the performing arts industries. Pete has managed shows throughout the UK and Europe for over a decade at venues including The Roundhouse, Hackney Empire, Schaubühne (Berlin), Birmingham Repertory Theatre, Soho Theatre, Liverpool Everyman, Battersea Arts Centre, Midlands Arts Centre, Birmingham O2 Academy, and Nottingham Playhouse.

Pete has also designed, built and run immersive experiences for clients, including Merlin Entertainment and The Tussauds Group.

He has toured and worked with musicians and artists worldwide for many years, including: Frank Carter & The Rattlesnakes, Shit Theatre, B Team, Sikth, We are The Ocean and Mallory Knox.

Theatre credits for the Bush include: *House of Ife, Sleepova*.

CHLOE WILSON | COMPANY STAGE MANAGER

Chloe Wilson is a Stage Management graduate from the Royal Central School of Speech and Drama. Her Company Stage Manager credits include: *Potted Panto* (Apollo/The Core, Corby Cube); *Trainspotting Live*, *Oi Frog and Friends! Live* (UK tours); *Straight White Men* (Southwark).

Her credits as Stage Manager include: *Echo Land* (Rich Mix); *Nevergreen* (Poplar Union); *A Silver Bell*, *Liminal*, *Clean @ 17*, *Death & Dancing* (King's Head); *The Mikado* (Maltings); *Juliet & Romeo* (Upstairs at The Gatehouse).

Her credits as Assistant Stage Manager include: *Windfall* (Southwark); *L'Enfant Prodigue*, *Passion*, *Poison & Petrifaction* (Susie Sainsbury Theatre, Royal Academy of Music).

SOPHIE HALIBURN | ASSISTANT STAGE MANAGER

Sophie Haliburn trained at Rose Bruford College in Stage Management.

Assistant Stage Management theatre credits include: *Sleepova* (Bush); *Reasons You Should(n't) Love Me*, *The Wife of Willesden*, *NW Trilogy*, *The Invisible Hand* (Kiln); *Bridgerton* (Secret Cinema).

Props Assistant theatre credits include: *Billy Elliot* (Leicester Curve); *Madhouse* (Ambassadors); *Oklahoma!* (Young Vic); *Translations*, *The Ocean at the End of the Lane*, *Mr. Gum and The Dancing Bear – The Musical!*, *If Not Now When?*, *Anna*, *Downstate* (National), *Orpheus and Eurydice*, *The Mask of Orpheus* (London Coliseum); *A Taste of Honey* (National Theatre tour).

Bush Theatre 50 EST. 1972

We make theatre for London. Now.

Celebrating its 50th Birthday, the Bush is a world-famous home for new plays and an internationally renowned champion of playwrights. We discover, nurture and produce the best new writers from the widest range of backgrounds from our home in a distinctive corner of west London.

The Bush has won over 100 awards and developed an enviable reputation for touring its acclaimed productions nationally and internationally.

We are excited by exceptional new voices, stories and perspectives – particularly those with contemporary bite which reflect the vibrancy of British culture now.

Located in the newly renovated old library on Uxbridge Road in the heart of Shepherd's Bush, the theatre houses two performance spaces, a rehearsal room and the lively Library Café & Bar.

Supported by
ARTS COUNCIL ENGLAND

h&f
hammersmith & fulham

bushtheatre.co.uk

Bush Theatre

Artistic Director	Lynette Linton
Executive Director (outgoing)	Lauren Clancy
Executive Director (incoming)	Mimi Findlay
Associate Artistic Director	Daniel Bailey
Development Assistant	Laura Aiton
Marketing Manager	Shannon Clarke
Literary Assistant	Amy Crighton
Head of Development & Marketing	Ruth Davey
Finance Assistant	Lauren Francis
Young Company Coordinator	Katie Greenall
Technical & Buildings Manager	Jamie Haigh
Head of Finance	Neil Harris
Marketing & Development Assistant	Laela Henley-Rowe
Assistant Producer	Nikita Karia
Community Assistant & Theatre Administrator	Joanne Leung
PA to the Executive	April Miller
Literary Manager	Deirdre O'Halloran
Producer	Oscar Owen
Event Sales Manager & Technician	Charlie Sadler
Venue Manager (Theatre)	Ade Seriki
Press Manager	Martin Shippen
Community Producer	Holly Smith
Marketing Manager	Ed Theakston
Development Officer	Eleanor Tindall
Venue Manager (Bar)	Adaeze Uyanwah
General Manager	Angela Wachner
Assistant Venue Manager (Box Office)	Robin Wilks

DUTY MANAGERS
Sara Dawood, Molly Elson, Nick Malkewitz & Dominic Taylor.

VENUE SUPERVISORS
Antony Baker & Judd Launder.

VENUE ASSISTANTS
Tabatha Batra Vaughan, Maryse Baya, Rowan Blake Prescott, William Byam-Shaw, Addy Caulder-James, Kane Feagan, Lydia Feerick, Matias Hailu, Anastasiya Hamolka, Rae Harm, Li Ikoku-Smith, Bo Leandro, Vanessa N'tshonso-Tchinda, Jennifer Okolo, Kyra Palma, Saroja-Lily Ratnavel, Coral Richards, Madeleine Simpson-Kent & Merle Wheldon-Posner.

BOARD OF TRUSTEES
Uzma Hasan (Chair), Kim Evans, Keerthi Kollimada, Lynette Linton, Rajiv Nathwani, Stephen Pidcock, Catherine Score & Cllr Mercy Umeh.

Bush Theatre, 7 Uxbridge Road, London W12 8LJ
Box Office: 020 8743 5050 | Administration: 020 8743 3584
Email: info@bushtheatre.co.uk | bushtheatre.co.uk

Alternative Theatre Company Ltd
The Bush Theatre is a Registered Charity
and a company limited by guarantee.
Registered in England no. 1221968 Charity no. 270080

THANK YOU

The Bush Theatre would like to thank all its supporters whose valuable contributions have helped us to create a platform for our future and to promote the highest quality new writing, develop the next generation of creative talent, lead innovative community engagement work and champion diversity.

Supported by
ARTS COUNCIL ENGLAND

If you are interested in finding out how to be involved, please visit **bushtheatre.co.uk/support-us**
email **development@bushtheatre.co.uk** or call **020 8743 3584**.

August in England

Lenny Henry has been a comedian since the age of sixteen. He has risen from being a cult star on children's television to becoming one of Britain's best known television performers, as well as a writer, philanthropist and award-winning stage actor. Lenny's recent screen credits include *The Witcher: Blood Origin*, *The Rings of Power*, *Broadchurch*, *The Syndicate* and the biographic film *Danny and the Human Zoo*. In theatre, Lenny has starred in *The Comedy of Errors* at the National Theatre, *Fences* at the Duchess Theatre and *The Resistable Rise of Arturo Ui* at the Donmar Warehouse.

As a co-founder and public face of *Comic Relief*, Lenny has played a central role in the charity, raising over £1 billion since 1985. He is a leading advocate for diversity in the arts and has established a Centre for Media Diversity at Birmingham City University, written two books on the topic and now has a podcast. He has been a Trustee of the National Theatre since February 2016, and was awarded a Knighthood in 2015 for services to drama and charity.

Lenny's production company, Douglas Road, has achieved success in partnership with Banijay, and has just finished co-producing his new ITV1 drama series *Three Little Birds*.

Lenny has written two memoirs with Faber, alongside a series of children's books published through Pan Macmillan.

LENNY HENRY

August in England

faber

First published in 2023
by Faber and Faber Limited
The Bindery, 51 Hatton Garden
London, ECIN 8HN

Typeset by Brighton Gray
Printed and bound in the UK by CPI Group (Ltd), Croydon CR0 4YY

A CIP record for this book
is available from the British Library

ISBN 978-0-571-38643-7

MIX
Paper | Supporting
responsible forestry
FSC® C013604

Printed and bound in the UK on FSC® certified paper in line with our continuing
commitment to ethical business practices, sustainability and the environment.
For further information see faber.co.uk/environmental-policy

Our authorised representative in the EU for product safety is
Easy Access System Europe, Mustamäe tee 50, 10621 Tallinn, Estonia
gpsr.requests@easproject.com

2 4 6 8 10 9 7 5 3

Acknowledgements

Thank you for buying this playtext/programme.

I want to say big respect to all the people that have made this play and the writing process possible. It's a whole heap a people.

Dig it.

Lynette Linton – Co-Director – big-up!
Daniel Bailey – Co-Director – big tings a gwarn . . .
Deirdre O'Halloran – Dramaturg – Uh-oh, D's thinking.
Chloe Wilson – Company Stage Manager – many thanks.
Sophie Haliburn – Assistant Stage Manager – blessings.
The Henrys and the Parkers – much love.

And massive respect to these guys too:
Natalie Pryce – Designer
Jai Morjaria – LD
Duramaney Kamara – Sound Designer
Gino Green – Video Deisgner
Shelley Maxwell – Movement Director
Hazel Holder – Voice & Dialect Coach
Male Arcucci – Costume Supervisor
Peter Rickards – Production Manager
Also – Peter Bennett-Jones my extraordinary manager
Abi Ribbans and Magdalene Bird
Rebecca Ptaszynski
Dennis Kelly
David Olusoga
Steve Bergson
Anna Steiner
Ellie Humphrey
Carole Emmett
Billie and Esme.

And of course, my rock, the fantastic Lisa Makin.

How *August in England* Came to Be

I'd spoken to Lynette Linton, the young powerhouse playwright and Artistic Director of the Bush Theatre, about three years ago. This was just before the first lockdown, 2020.

I'd written a couple plays for the BBC and the odd screenplay. Talking to Lynette empowered me, made me feel that there were things to say and do about what was going on right now. And what was going on right now – at that time anyway – was the Windrush Scandal.

Amelia Gentleman had been sustaining a bravura national conversation with some of the victims of the Home Office's pernicious and cruel machinations. She wrote a piece about a former chef called Paulette Wilson, who had been employed at the House of Commons. She had been told, categorically, that because she had never applied for a British passport (she had come to the UK in 1968), she had no papers proving she had a right to be in the UK. Shortly after, Gentleman interviewed Anthony Bryan, who was in the same dire situation.

Theresa May's hostile environment had slowly solidified into a kind of best practice, placing at risk approximately 57,000 people. Although they had come to Britain from a Commonwealth country before 1971, because they had never applied for a British passport or been naturalised, they were in danger of being tossed out of the UK and sent back to a home country they hadn't revisited for many years.

I was moved by this predicament.

I wanted to do something to help.

Lynette suggested I channel these feelings into a play or monologue.

Which is exactly what I did. I wrote *August in England* in New Zealand, while playing a Harfoot in *The Rings of Power*. I tapped away while waiting to destroy the original

Witcher universe in a TV series called *Blood Origin*. I even worked on the script while waiting to shoot my two scenes on Lynette's debut TV film, *My Name Is Leon*.

It's been a long revision process, sometimes on hold while I wrote another post-Windrush drama for ITV called *Three Little Birds*, inspired by my family's stories of coming to the UK in the mid-fifties.

My point, and I do have one, is that I wanted to tell a story about a guy who was born in Jamaica, came to Britain in the fifties on his mum's passport, and had a life in the UK. Fifty-two years of paying taxes, working his socks off and being a citizen.

The hostile environment affected many people. August Henderson is just one of them.

Hope you enjoy the play.

Sir Lenny Henry
London, March 2023

With thanks to Lynette Linton, Daniel Bailey, Amelia Gentleman and Anna Steiner and David Olusoga and everyone who helped to make *August in England* happen.

August in England was first performed on 28 April 2023 at the Bush Theatre, London, with the following cast:

August Henderson Lenny Henry

Co-Directors Daniel Bailey and Lynette Linton
Set and Costume Designer Natalie Pryce
Lighting Designer Jai Morjaria
Sound Designer and Composer Duramaney Kamara
Video Designer Gino Ricardo Green
Movement Director Shelley Maxwell
Voice and Dialect Coach Hazel Holder
Dramaturg Deirdre O'Halloran
Windrush Consultant Amelia Gentleman
Costume Supervisor Malena Arcucci
Production Manager Pete Rickards for eStage
Company Stage Manager Chloe Wilson
Assistant Stage Manager Sophie Haliburn

Character

August Henderson
black, sixties

AUGUST IN ENGLAND

Note

August code-switches from Jamaican (*JA*)
to Black Country (*BC*) throughout.

*

wor – won't

cor – can't

day – didn't

shore – shan't

ent – ain't

cowin' – like 'bloody' or 'flipping'

ONE

*We're in a living room – there's a concealed screen upon
which images will be played.*

*This begins as August Henderson (black, sixties) chills and
chats in his safe environment, but will alter at various stages
throughout the show until we are somewhere inhospitable.*

*Right now, as the lights rise – there's a nice vibe here –
August chats to people as they come in, offers them rum or a
tin of beer – it feels like a celebration.*

*There's music playing: 'Jump in the Line' by Harry
Belafonte, 'Independent Jamaica' by Lord Creator, 'Welcome
to Jamrock' by Damian Marley.*

Yu see me? I was eight years old when I come to H'Inglan' –
I travel on my mother's passport; Jamaica was a British
colony back then – we could go anywhere in the empire.
They even split Jamaica into three counties: Cornwall,
Middlesex and Surrey.

But if you go to Cornwall in Jamaica and yu want a pasty?
Don't say – (*English*) 'I'd like to purchase a *pasty* please' –
you haffe say – (*JA*) 'Gimme seventeen *pattie* nuh? An' move
yuself – mi have tings fe do.'

This was early 1962. Before Jamaican independence.

So. My dad – they call him Hubert Henderson . . . cos that
was his *name* –

He went to England two years or so before to, in his words:
(*JA*) 'Look fe work and find somewhere decent for all of us
to live an' start this godforsaken life again.'

That was the *plan.*

That's what he told Mama anyway. *He'd* go to England, *cos he was the man*: then once he was set up, me and Mama – *she* was called Tallulah Henderson – we'd travel by plane from Jamaica to London and hallelujah! we'd be a family reunited.

(*BC*) Now back in the day my papa was not the only man to make a plan like that. He was also not the only man to make a complete bollocks of that plan. *He get it so wrong.*

He was supposed to send for us in 1961.

He never did though – Papa never sent for us. No boat or plane tickets. Not even one an' two planks and a couple of oars.

Mum gave up waiting in the end. By spring 1962 she was like: (*JA*) 'Dat's it – find me suitcase, me a go t' H'Ingland.'

So, *my* mama borrow money from *her* mama – Granny Curtis.

Tiny lickle bend-up bend-up woman wid a wrinkle-up wrinkle-up face – look like so: (*Does her face.*) NOW – she tell Mama to leave Jamaica and tek me too – said it would do me good.

(*JA*) 'Tallulah yu mad? Yu cyaan leave August here wid me – the boy too rude. He need his poopa. Yu have to bend the tree when it young; if yu wait till it's old it wi' jus' bruk' off in yu hand.'

She was sayin' that Dad would have to teach me right from wrong *early* – otherwise by the time I reached my teens I'd be Scarface – green banana in one hand, jerk chicken leg in the other: 'Say hello to my liddle friends!'

Mama wrote to Papa, I remember her sat there with the blue air mail paper and a leaky biro – (*JA*) 'Dear Hubert. Me an' August soon come. Meet us at the h'airport in London at the time stated below. Kind regards – Tallulah.'

And that was us. On the next BOAC flight to Blighty – the mother country – H'Ingland.

We soon reach London Airport: my hair's combed, my skin's shiny with Vaseline – so are my shoes.

Mama's in her brand-new wig!

She's wearin' the sticky-out church frock. She looks good.

We walk down the steps from the plane – full of hope, through customs, out the other side to be met by –

Pause.

Nobody.

Absolutely no one.

Nobody waving handmade signs sayin': (*JA*) 'Tallulah and August Henderson – yu reach!'

Or: (*JA*) 'Welcome to H'Inglan' – dis way for streets paved wid gold! Honest to God.'

And definitely – no Dad; no bloody husband to meet-and-greet us either.

The secret word of the day was 'Hu-mili-ay-shon'.

A letter slips under his door. Brown envelope – he opens it, reads it. Puts it to one side.

TWO

Dad was stayin in this godawful bedsit in the ass-end of London – a place called Peckham.

And I know it's all 'Cushty, Del Boy, chandelier, mangetout, mangetout, lovely jubbly' now.

But back *then*? Back in the early sixties – mek me tell yu someting . . . Peckham was *rough*!

(*JA*) Puss 'fraid a rat cos dem carry machete! Rough!

So we got three buses – took nearly four and a half hours to get to where Dad was – when we reach the front door, the landlady let us in and Mum just took off, charged upstairs two steps at a time, I thought the devil was on her heels.

Soon as Mama opened the door – I *knew* something wasn't right. First thing was the smell comin' out of that room. Oh my God – the *stench* of it – it's still in my nostrils. It was sweat and Guinness and whiffy feet and Park Drive cigarettes – like being stuck in a lift with Bernard Manning.

Mama was cryin' even before she'd set foot in the room.

Papa was – he was – he was *with* somebody.

She was a very good-looking woman as well, y'know? But she was . . . unkempt. She looked like she hadn't been *kempt* since the night before.

She was a redhead.

She had red lips.

Pale white skin.

Freckles.

Stunning.

I was eight. You don't forget someone like her.

Mama went ballistic. Ever see a Jamaican woman fight for her man?

He removes imaginary jewellery.

(JA) 'Oh? Yu tink I jus' gwine let yu teef my husband? In front o' me? *My* husband?

'Mek me jus' Vaseline mi face an tek off mi ears ring – alright. Come nuh!'

The redhead flew out the room so quick she left one of her stilettos behind.

18

Mum picked it up, opened the window, waited for her to come out the front door and dash the shoe after her – PLAPS! (JA) 'Catch my woman right in her neck back!'

A couple more envelopes are stuffed under the door. He picks them up – opens one – reads it – puts it with the others.

THREE

That was the end of Hubert and Tallulah – or it certainly felt like an ending to me. She told Dad to bugger off . . . he did, and we managed on our own.

We began new lives in Peckham – lived on Calypso Crescent –

Calypso music plays momentarily – he moves to the rhythm.

Yes man! Calypso Crescent . . .

Music stops.

It was a shithole but Mum *liked* the name so that was that.

And after a while, Dad came creepin' back, said he was sorry and he'd never do it again. Mama forgave him. And then he did it again! At least twice more and – she kept *forgiving him.*

That's why I never married Clarice.

(JA) A serf-e-ticket from some vicar wasn't gonna make me stay faithful. Only *we* could do that.

Time trot by.

Mum had this idea that we should move up to the Midlands.

(JA) 'It cheaper to live up there and them have plenty, plenty black people, a whole heap a factory an' not too much pressure.'

I guess she figured she had to get Dad away from London or there'd be a queue of redheads outside the door day and night and she'd have to keep boxing them down from dawn till dusk.

We moved up to the Jewel of the Midlands. They call it: (*Posh*) 'Sandwell' now but when we first got there everybody called it: (*BC*) 'West Bromwich' . . .

I went to St Mark's Junior School – I've got all the photographs somewhere – y'know when they do that big group shot of the entire school? In every single one, I'm the tiny black smudge over on the left by the kitchens. You couldn't see me! But I'm there!

After the first few years, Mama even made me bring a torch – (*JA*) 'I'm not buyin' one more photo unless mi can see you!'

(*JA*) White pickneys used to pick on me – call me all kindsa names – (*Full-on Jamaican*) But dem don't know me.

Yu see me?

Mi name August Chamberlain Henderson – born a Jamaica!

I put a stop to all that name-callin' foolishness quick sharp!

Before dem can even move dem mout' to say coon or nigger or wog – I would jus' tump dem down wid whatever was nearby!

Tree branch.

Lamp post.

Volkswagen.

Dis one pickney Paul Murphy? Call me a '*stinkin' blackie*'.

'Blackie', y'know? Humph – I tink him did seh '*Bla*—' before I jam a stickle brick in him left eyeball! PLAP!

I did jook him y'see?

Wasn't *that* serious.

He had to wear one of them big eyepatches till the sixth year.

I see him up town sometimes. He dun't see me tho.

Specially if I'm on the left-hand side of the street . . .

So that's where I did the rest of me growin' up. The Black Country – home of West Bromwich Albion! 'Come on you baggies! Boing boing!'

The refrain from 'Liquidator' by Harry J Allstars plays – August chants 'West Brom!' after the hand claps.

FOUR

The white kids at school was always pokin' me in the chest in the playground: (BC) 'August. How comes you'm always talkin' Jamaican? Yow'm here now – y've gorra spake the Queen's English now ay ya!'

I never knew what they were on about. We used to watch the Queen's Speech every Christmas – she never once come on and went: (BC) 'Alright how'm ya gooin? We'm gonna have a bostin' year this year ay we?'

Never happened.

When I went to Bilston Senior School, there were more black kids there. What a relief. We made friends – most of us did – formed gangs. Safety in numbers I suppose. It was great having new friends – we liked the same tings . . . we laughed at the same jokes – we were having the best of both worlds – we rocked the West Indian *and* the West Bromwich lifestyle.

We did things all the *other* yout's were doing *back then* . . .

We all tried weed, but these were Black Country spliffs – you never quite got high *enough*. You'd get maybe halfway and then a mate'd have to give you a leg-up. We watched *Top of the Pops* and we'd listen to Bob Marley and Toots and the Maytals – be like (BC) 'Why can't *we* be revolutionary like these guys?'

So we formed a band.

We ran tings like dis!

On drums: Stixman Lincoln Barton – couldn't keep time to save his life but his dad had a Ford Transit so he was in.

On bass we had Cleveland 'Dry Back Foot' Edwards – we called him that cos he never moisturised his feet. He was a disgrace.

Rockin the ryddim guitar was Ramgoat Rodney Livingstone – he thought he was a ladies' man. Every time we played, he'd try hard to make love to the guitar and each time the guitar would go: (*Brum*) 'Ramgoat? I've gotta headache.'

Then there was Marcus Marsh: The Revolutionary Dread on co-lead vocals and keyboards – we called him 'The Revolutionary' cos he wanted to burn down Babylon – but only after *Match of the Day*.

Finally, there was me – August Henderson on lead vocals and charisma. I was the Black Country's Bob Marley.

(*Sings*)
I shot the sheriff –
But I day shoot the deputy –
it wor me, I was in The Coach and Horses . . .
Eating a bag of pork scratchin's . . .
With me nan.

This was early seventies – a time of skinheads and the National Front and 'Keep Britain White' – they hated us.

It was weird: they had the same short haircuts and skinny-leg trousers just like we did. They loved reggae and ska in the beginning, but *after a while*, they stopped loving us. I still don't know what changed.

These National Front skinheads came down the youth club one night and tried to burn the place down. While we were on stage.

One genius filled a bottle with paraffin and then stuffed newspaper in the top. He musta spilt paraffin over himself and never noticed. Cos when he lit the newspaper? His whole sleeve went up in flames – he ran off screaming: 'I'm on cowin' fire! Me bastard jacket's on FIRE!'

They were so embarrassed they never came back.

We called the band Black Fist cos it sounded militant. It didn't matter that all of us lived with our parents and wore second-hand clothes, we was militant!

In our minds we were tougher than tough! We were the Black Panthers and Malcolm X and Kunta Kinte from *Roots* all rolled into one.

People liked Black Fist – everybody was coming to see us. Kids, teachers, parole officers . . . it was a diverse audience. I've still got the clippings from the *Express* and *Star* – the headline was – 'You Can't Resist Black Fist!' I wrote underneath – 'Especially if you're pissed . . .'

I used to love singing 'Twistin' the Night Away' by Sam Cooke – we did a ska version –

He makes percussive ska-type noises with his mouth, and sings the chorus of the song.

Marcus hated them songs. Said we sounded too happy.

He was like: (*JA*) 'How we supposed to overcome Babylon singin' about "The Twist" to raas claat!'

I used to say: 'Marcus? All I wanna do is make a few quid and find a girl to snog me lips off and dance so close you couldn't slide a library card between us – that's all I want.'

Then he said: (*JA*) 'Who would want to snog you, August Henderson? You is a hugly raatid claat bumbo hole!'

And he'd walk out.

He had no idea.

FIVE

Time's rolling now.

And we'd been going a while; playin' school discos, youth clubs; The Roots and Culture Centre in Smethwick. Sounds nice dunt it? Y'think you'm getting' paid proper and then after the gig, you come out and some bastard's nicked the tyres off the van.

We got a few pub and club gigs as far away as Coventry . . . We thought we were gonna be huge.

And Clarice would always be there at the front – raising her fist in the air, and just occasionally taking her eyes off the front of me trousers to look me in the face. Her smile was gorgeous. I liked her straight away – she had this deep voice.

Clarice grew up with elder brothers and sisters who'd just refused to integrate and speak like everyone else in West Bromwich – her house was like the Jamaican embassy. Bob Marley woulda walked in and gone: (JA) 'Why people cyaan talk H'Inglish in dis ya house?'

We got on really well. I loved everyting about her . . .

Fantastic full lips – beautiful toes – always well-manicured. She wasn't snaggly and jagged like Wolverine down there.

And she loved to read – I mean everything from the *Jackie* to *Jane Eyre* to bell hooks – the woman read everyting.

Best thing of all? We made each other *laugh*.

And back then – all of us were trying to figure out how to be in this country, cos trying to have some kind of identity as a young black man in the late seventies was tough.

In the club when I was dancing with Clarice, my top half was Black Country but the bottom half was pure Jamaican – y'overstan'?

We'd wind our hips against each other – like this – *for hours* (*JA*) slow wine we call it.

A way of dancing . . . that was as close to having actual sex . . . as humanly possible.

Me an' Clarice was like fire. FIRE!

Then one night after a show she said: (*JA, deep*) 'August?'

Honestly – her voice drove me mad.

She said: (*JA*) 'August? Yu know I love you, right?'

And I nodded, cos – she knows *I* love *her* . . .

She goes: (*JA*) 'Good, because mi have someting to say an yu might not like it.'

I'm like: 'Has Ramgoat tried to put the moves on you again? I'll knock his cowin' block off.'

She goes: (*JA*) 'It's not that. It's this. Black Fist is never gonna make it big in the music industry. Yu don't write yu own songs – you only just play yu instruments and *you're* the only good-lookin' one. The rest o' yu ugly like mongoose wid a migraine.'

There's such a thing as too much honesty.

She goes on:

(*JA*) 'No record company people comin' to see yu – thirty pound split five ways, minus two pound each for petrol – whatever leave won't even buy yu a packet of chewing gum, let alone a lickle cottage in Negril. *And* you're at the factory all day – out with the band every night.'

I was crushed – I had tears in me eyes – but she hadn't finished:

(*JA*) 'August? If we goin' to be in this together – *have children*, all dat? I need to know, *you* understand we're goin' to need structure and stability . . . Because if we don't have dem tings? This relationship done.'

I stopped cryin' – why's she keep talkin' about *family*?

And then I got it –

He sings the first two lines of 'A Message to You, Rudy' by The Specials.

I told Marcus and the rest of 'em – we took all the instruments down the pawn shop, sold everythin', divvied up the money and went our separate ways. *Black Fist was done.*

We needed as much money as we could get at this point with Clarice pregnant, so I took on extra shifts to make more money.

When I started at the factory – Dad and his mates took the piss out of me: weldin' me boots to the floor, sendin' me to the stores for a left-handed spanner, or a sky hook – Hilarious – I don't think. Dad could see it was getting to me at the time, but he never did nothing. Later on though, when they made me a supervisor, he backed off.

(*JA*) He had to or I woulda sack him backside!

Besides I didn't have time for his nonsense now – I had other things to worry about: like was I gonna marry Clarice *or* not? (*JA*) Dat was the million-dollar question!

I never wanted to get married: My thinking was – Mum and Dad were married and look where it got them? Miserable as Nigel Farage at Notting Hill Carnival.

Clarice agreed – she said: (*JA*) 'If you don't get married you can't get divorced' . . . I liked her thinking.

So instead of all that *love, honour and obey* malarkey – me and Clarice had a party – a massive dance! With rum punch, pie and peas, curry goat and rice, Banks's bitter and pork scratchings. Babycham and Cherry B for the ladies. Rum fe the mandem!

We had a soundsystem so big you could see it from Jupiter.

It was a bostin' party. Everybody was there (*JA*) an' we mash up the place cos we was happy.

You can see Clarice's baby bump in all the pictures – we look over-the-moon happy – because we are. Louise was our first. She was perfect. The missing piece in our jigsaw puzzle.

From the minute I held her in my arms – I knew.

Louise was the saving of me – and it wouldn't be the last time.

Meanwhile – back at work I'd made a friend – Iqbal. He's a good bloke. He's Indian. Whenever me and Iqbal get a break – he'd smoke cigarettes and we'd sit and talk about working together in the future. Iqbal's uncle had a grocery shop up town.

Iqbal kept sayin' me and him could run his uncle's business so much better than him. Iqbal could do all the behind-the-scenes – organising, ordering stuff, paperwork, talking to wholesalers. And I'd be up front with the customers, making them laugh and smile and buying an extra six pounds of yam.

We talked about the amount of black people in the Midlands – target them and then steer them away from the corporate supermarkets.

We had some good ideas and in the end, we decided to go for it.

It was the right time. I was a father now, and we wanted more kids. A whole heap a pickney.

I wanted to provide for their future. I wanted Louise to be proud of her dad.

I also wanted to be in charge of something for a change.

Something that was mine.

I'd been in the band but Marcus was in charge of that.

I'd worked in a factory – but *Dad* ran things there for ages – his smell was all over everything. Everywhere I went.

I didn't want that 'dad smell' around *me* anymore.

I'd been saving money to put into our new business venture:

AUGUST AND IQBAL'S FRUIT AND VEG EMPORIUM.

It was 'GO BIG OR GO HOME' time. I was excited; I told Iqbal, 'Come on, let's do it, let's buy the shop from your uncle – what we waiting for?'

Now – Iqbal had a fair bit of money put away, he was ready, but I was nowhere near.

So I went and talked to my mom and dad about a loan.

Mum made me eat first, obviously.

(*JA*) She cook Saturday soup – and it was Thursday! Mutton and dumplin' and yam and potato and carrots and garlic and thyme . . . I hadn't eaten like that since the Saturday before.

Dad poured me a Guinness. I don't know how he does it but he always gets the white bit on the bottom. How is that even possible?

Once we'd eaten I told them what me and Iqbal was doin' and how much it would be and what it would mean to be my own boss at last.

They never said nothing. Dad just did this:

He sucks his teeth.

Mum kept schtum.

I imagined them laughing at me as soon as I was out the front door:

(*JA*) 'How much him want? For a fruit an' veg shop? Call the lunatic asylum! How yu goin' sell yam and breadfruit to H'Inglish people? All dem eat is fish an' chips! August gone crazy!'

Weeks go by.

I'm sweating. Iqbal's being cool about it, but I can see he wants to jus' get going and I'm holding him back. Iqbal's my best mate, I don't wanna let him down.

Then this one day, I go for a pre-Sunday-lunch drink with me dad down The Shakespeare's Arms – he buys me a Guinness and slips me a brown envelope. There's a big wad of cash in there. I can't believe it. He looks at me and says: (*JA*) 'Don't tell you moomah.'

Saturday after that – Mama comes round after bingo up town. Clarice lets her in.

And then goes: (*JA*) 'August! Yu mama downstairs!'

I run down to say hi – and she gives me this big wink, reaches in her purse and gives me this thick white envelope – she goes: (*JA*) 'Tom Mix, number six – don't tell yu poopah.'

And that was it! Iqbal and me were now the proud owners of August and Iqbal's Fruit and Veg Emporium.

Quite a large space off of Edwards Hill just round by the dairy. Big garden with a wooden shed in it – I say garden . . . Nobody'd taken care of it for ages. It looked like Dunkirk the day after.

But we didn't care – we'd managed to get hold of this great place where there's room for all the fruit, veg and tinned goods anybody could ever wish for. We was in business.

Fillin' out all the paperwork's a ball-ache, but you gotta ent ya? And there was things like tax forms to fill out; insurance and pension stuff – and I wanna get it right – *I've got to* – (*JA*) *I am now half of the incredibly handsome: August and Iqbal's Fruit and Veg Emporium – to backside: Get in!*

SIX

After a while Lawrence came along – it was a long birthing process.

Eighteen hours. When he come out, he had sideburns. I sat with Clarice for ages after he was born and she was knackered – she looked at me and said: (*JA*) 'No more baby after dis one, alright? We don't need to breed no football team.'

When Louise was little, she was always trying to help her mum. One day she picked Lawrence up out of his bed and he slipped out of her hands and fell head-first onto the lino. He never cried or nothing – didn't even say 'Mama' – I'm surprised he never bounced.

Lawrence, man. Even as a little kid – he was a bad man! Disobedient? Lord Jesus Christ. He never had to go outside and look fe trouble. There'd be a knock on the front door – Trouble'd be right there: 'Hello, Mr Henderson – we found this old box of hand grenades and a battery-operated chainsaw just lying in the gutter – does Lawrence want to come out and play?'

All I remember is Louise getting straight As an' bein' a model pupil – and always in the head teacher's office cos Lawrence bite somebody . . . usually a prefect.

When he was twelve he teef Clarice car! I'm not lyin'! Police catch him at Spaghetti Junction.

I did beat him for that. It put pressure on the marriage. Because Clarice and I never agree on how to raise him. But I remember what Granny Curtis say about raisin' a boy child. I had to bend the tree young because if wait till it get too old, it will bruk in two. I didn't want to bruk Lawrence so I decide to talk to him. I ask him what would make him happy. He say he want a driving job. That would make him happy.

So I teach him to drive the car on Safeway's car park. He pass his test first time. He's a full-time bus driver now. He like to mess wid the passengers – turn on the microphone and go:

'Ladies and gentlemen: We won't be stopping at the next destination because the brakes have gone!'

Daft bugger.

Pause.

Where was I? Oh yes. Well when Clarice say: (*JA*) 'No more babies', she meant it.

(*JA*) 'NO MORE BABIES! Y'hear me August? Imagine it's rainin' in yu Y-fronts and put on a damn raincoat to raatid.'

So we practised safe sex all the time.

Which is why Georgie was such a big surprise. Seventeen years it took him. I knew he was going to be a good footballer – this boy know how to get past a rock-solid defence.

One minute Clarice was in the living room saying she's got *wind*. The next, she's in Maternity screaming for *pethidine*.

Mind you, to be fair, so was I.

And he's grown up to be such a good lad. He's a footballer and I'm so proud of him.

We christened him 'George, Pele, Cyrille, Laurie, Brendan, Nobby, Henderson'; that's a bostin' name. You'd never get it on the back of a shirt though.

I used to make him watch videos of George Best and Pele all the time.

August is watching footy with Georgie.

(*JA*) 'Now, watch Pele, son – watch what he do – he pass the ball to my man's left and then run all the way past him on the right and pick up the ball, nutmeg two a dem and then . . .'

August gets up.

'BOOM – SHAKA – LAKA!

GOOOOAAAAAAAAAAAAAAAAAAAAAAAAALLLL!'

Throws baby in the air.

SEVEN

You gotta watch time y'know? Time fast, to raatid.

One minute you got three kids, all different: one of 'em outside hoovering the backyard, the youngest's practising corner kicks in the kitchen, and the middle one's in the front room . . . planning a bank job.

And then – it's over, all the school runs, the trips to the head teacher's office, the freezing cold school football matches . . . all done and dusted.

Louise is married, Lawrence has got his own place, Georgie's at the West Brom under-eighteens.

Mama died. She wanted the full service, nine hymns and a procession. Then another service by the graveside.

We buried her at Sandwell Valley Cemetery. It was good.

Some of her church friends helped to shovel the dirt.

(*Sings*)
Mi glory glory, mi hallelujah, when I lay my burden down
Mi glory glory, mi hallelujah, when I lay my burden down.

It took ages – the white man with the JCB was right there – he was vex yu see?

We sang three more songs – and then it was done. Mama had a good send-off.

Wasn't long after that when Dad went. Last week he was alive, I saw him every day. He just wanted to talk and talk and talk – he said:

(*JA*) 'When I first came to H'Ingland – it was like white people would just ignore me in the street, like I didn't exist, like they didn't see me. It mek me mad.'

Two days later he was dead.

Papa never want to be buried so we cremate him. He said:

(*JA*) 'Afterlife? Listen – wherever I'm goin? It's gonna be warm – might as well get on with it.'

And then it was just me an' Clarice, on our own, in the house.

And once it was just us it was . . . *easy* y'know?

We had all this time on our own – nobody else around.

It was good times. Listening to music – Clarice never learns the words: 'Say my name, say my name – shemma shemma baby, shemma shemma maybe – all you do is shemma name' – what kind of lyrics is that?

We had fun though. It was just us. Living life, y'know?

But one day . . .

I notice, Clarice is losing weight . . .

I never said nothin'.

But it was noticeable y'know?

We're talkin' Oprah, Beyoncé, Diana Ross in the space of two months.

I tried to make her eat more. Iqbal played a blinder here. Once a week got Raani his missus to make chana and saag and mutter paneer and aloo gobi and chicken jalfrezi for us – But she wouldn't eat – she'd completely lost her appetite –

And then . . . and then . . . she had blood in her . . . in her . . .

And couple times . . . she couldn't breathe properly.

From then onwards she was backward an' forward having all these treatments and medication. Chemo. Radiotherapy.

She was really under the weather – and that's when – that's when . . .

I think I lost my mind for a bit. I mean, I didn't go completely loo-lah – I ent even got the right words for it

I felt really terrible; as down as anyone could be.

And don't get me wrong, how *I* was feeling was nowhere near as painful as what Clarice was going through – ut that doesn't mean I wasn't in serious pain – (*Taps temple.*) up here.

I really was.

I was supporting Clarice the best way I could . . . rushin' home from work, preparin' her food, makin' sure she was taking her meds at the right times.

I had to organise everything. I was there for her. But we were both down.

    Pause.

We'd stopped bein' . . . intimate.

She was sick, man . . . And I missed her . . . the closeness of her.

The shop was getting busy. Sometimes, it was too much. We couldn't afford any more staff.

Louise did her best to help out though. She's a teacher and bright like her mother. She's good at all that admin stuff – paperwork, bookkeeping, that kind of thing.

Her husband's an ex-convict. He was Brian when he went into jail but Rakim when he come out. He put on size in there. Built like a house with a beard.

(*JA*) He used to do breakin' and enterin' all over the Midlands. But dem catch him backside. He turn his life round tho.

Everybody say: 'Why Louise marry a ex-convict?' and I say –
(*JA*) 'He make some stupid mistakes but him done wid dat
now. Yu never mek a mistake?' Louise love him from when
she was seventeen – He's responsible now.

I tell him: 'Do right by Louise an' I will do right by you – yu
overstand? Him say, 'I overstand, Mr Henderson,' an' we
shake. Him so strong him nearly mash up me hand.

Rakim's teachin' Bums, Mums and Tums at the Fit Pit in
Wednesbury now.

My God, he's fit – you could bounce a bag of two-pound
coins off his abs.

Time galloping – we're about 2012.

Theresa May on TV talkin' about 'creatin' a hostile
environment for illegal immigration'. Have you seen Theresa
May dance? Now *that's* a hostile environment . . . she can
clear a dance floor quicker than foot an' mout' disease.

Clarice was getting beat up by the –

Pause.

She was gettin' worse – every day – I mean, sicker and sicker.
And it put me in a position. Without her wages coming in
every week, we were missing her contribution.

That's when Iqbal took me by the shoulders and give me a
good kick up the backside . . . He said it was my fault.

(*British South Asian*) 'August! You got a face like a well-
slapped arsehole.

'We got to get you happy – I can't have you miserable
around the shop!

'Look. I think people need music and alcohol and *fun* – like a
club or something. We could do it here: to get them through
the weekend!

35

'It'll make everyone happy – but most importantly – it'll cheer *you* up.'

I love Iqbal – even though he drives me crazy. This was one of his better ideas. So me and him started this – lickle members-only club – nutten fancy – it was at the back of the shop. Few drinks, some dominoes, music, food. Fi we.

It was gonna work. His dad knew somebody on the council who could make all the paperwork go away. We got a drinks licence. It all happened really quickly.

We called it 'The Back Room' because that's where it was, *INNA DE BACK ROOM!*

It was perfect. People started coming and it got popular – they liked it.

EIGHT

Loads of people started hanging out there – all through word of mouth.

One night: this woman comes in . . . with a friend of Iqbal's – she's drinkin' – laughin' and she's got:

Bright red hair.

Red lipstick.

Pale white skin.

She's stunning. Wearing a tight sparkly dress; way too fancy – like she was at a nightclub in Monte Carlo instead of a back room in West Bromwich that smells of turnips.

They called her Roisin.

She saw me looking a couple of times. I could tell she was Interested. But I'm . . . I'm taken. I've got Clarice to look after – I don't want –

Pause.

. . . she was going through all the chemo . . . the endless treatments . . . I was there for all of it.

Roisin was funny. She held the entire room in the palm of her hand . . .

(*Dublin*) 'A travellin' salesman knocks on a door; little boy answers.

'He's wearing a negligee, he's got a cigar in one hand and a bottle of whiskey in the other.

'The salesman says, "Is your mammy or daddy at home?"

'Little boy says:

'"The feck do you think?"'

She was a natural. And whether I wanted to or not – I couldn't keep away from her.

Music plays: 'Key to the World' by Ruddy Thomas.

We'd flirt and have the odd slow dance at the club . . . and at first – that's all it was . . . it was nothing.

Clarice was still uppermost in my mind . . . but this was something else.

Next thing I know, Roisin's *helping out* at The Back Room 'n' all – being the life and soul of the party. Making me laugh. Cheering me up. It was nice. She'd be there with her jokes:

(*Dublin*) 'Two goldfish in a tank. One of 'em says – "Jaysus, how d'ya drive this feckin' thing?"'

Roisin's irresistable. She's a super-electro magnet and I'm a bin bag full of iron filings.

Meanwhile . . . Clarice starts waking up at midnight wonderin' where I am.

And the truth was, I was with Roisin – and we were getting closer and closer to actually *doing* something about it.

37

I'd convinced myself in my head that nothing was *gonna* happen, but our bodies were having a different conversation. My brain's like: (*BC*) 'No no no no nope, no way!'

And my body's like: (*JA*) 'Where yu goin' darlin'? Hold on nuh – yu dress look nice . . .'

Then Lawrence did something – and I wish he'd never done it.

Whenever I was at home Clarice could see – she could tell – I wasn't as down as I'd been before.

I mean, I wasn't butt-naked and turning cartwheels, with a rose between me teeth – but she knew there'd been a change in me and that the club and whatever was going on there, was *part* of that change.

She was happy for me. Happy that I was happy.

So, this one night, she asked Lawrence to drive her down to inna de back room so she can see *what's making me so happy*.

Lawrence puts her in the car and drives her down to the club and escorts her in.

Music plays: 'Believe in Love' by Peter Hunnigale.

And that's when Clarice saw me and Roisin slow dancing, against the wall. Eyes closed. Lost.

She turned round and asked Lawrence to take her home.

Pause.

When she reach, Clarice got into bed and turned her face to the wall.

A week later she was dead.

NINE

Clarice's funeral was . . . it was lovely actually. Really big turn-out – everyone was . . .

The guys from Black Fist came to pay tribute. They wanted to do a ninety-minute set. I had to have a word with 'em – we'd only booked the crem for half an hour – they're really strict about timings.

In the end they did a medley of 'Redemption Song' and 'I Shot the Sheriff'.

They wanted to come back and do 'Feeling Hot Hot Hot' – but I put me foot down.

Everybody in the family was there – Louise, Rakim and their hyperactive kids Casper and William. Rakim choose dem names – when he was still called Brian.

Louise helped me to organise it all. Actually, she didn't just *help* – she did everything.

I was in no fit state to organise Clarice's funeral.

Lawrence wouldn't even look at me . . .

And Georgie was there of course. Destroyed.

He loved his mum so much. Spoke to her every day.

He never kept anything from her – when he got released from West Brom, he begged her to tell me for him – cos he knew *I'd* be upset.

Clarice was . . . golden.

Georgie cried all the way through her eulogy . . . there wasn't a dry eye in the house.

He had a mate with him – same age – one of the admin guys from up the football . . . He seemed just as upset as Georgie was.

Roisin showed up. I froze.

Lawrence recognised her straight away –

He said: (*BC, deep*) 'Get out! Right this minute! I mean now!'

Roisin was like: (*Dublin*) 'I just wanted to pay my respects.'

Louise jumped right down her throat – (*BC*) '"Respects?" You shouldn't even be in the *vicinity*! Leave. NOW!'

I couldn't . . . I didn't know what to say to her.

It was too much.

Roisin turned and walked away quickly. Redhead. Pale skin. Freckles. Red lipstick. Stunning . . . And then she was gone . . .

The pastor said a few words and then the curtains closed and Clarice's coffin disappeared behind them. Taking my heart with her.

Afterwards, Roisin kept callin' me – tryin' to cheer me up with jokes on me answerphone. But I couldn't bear it. So . . . I chucked the mobile away and got a new one. Done means done.

And this was the moment when Iqbal was making all sorts of random decisions to do with the shop. He open a daytime crèche – but him never hire any staff to look after the pickney dem. There was unsupervised toddlers walkin' round drinking salad dressing from the bottle, teefin' frozen fish out the freezer an' lickin' 'em like a choc ice. I put a stop to dat.

He wanted to open an internet café but he kept forgetting the shop's Wi-Fi password.

He bought these dodgy fireworks off Marky Yip up Scargill Street near the town centre.

It was what Marky called 'a job lot' – and they all got stuffed in the shed out the back. It's got a broken window at the side . . . but apart from that it's secure.

He goes: (*British South Asian, all happy*) 'August, mate –
this – is a bonfire night opportunity, just waiting to happen?
We'll be rich!'

(*JA*) The bloody eediat!

He stays in the chair – becomes depressed.

I fall deeper and deeper into this bottomless pit of grief.

Not only that – I had this dull pain in my head – day in day
out.

THOOM THOOM THOOM.

And I'm missing Clarice so . . . much . . .

Not only that: I've also got a mad bastard of a toothache.

This toothache was excruciating.

Part of me was thinking, 'Well, maybe you deserve this,
August.'

Because of what you put Clarice through. What she saw.

. . . So I decided to endure it – THOOM THOOM THOOM.

I spent months like this – I didn't care about anything that
was goin' on, I was just drifting through things. It was me
birthday – I didn't go to the party – Louise organised it and
she was vex with me for a week.

Nelson Mandela died. The funeral come on the telly and
I turned it off.

The kids organised Clarice's memorial service – I went to that.
I don't know how I got through it – I was so upset, it was the
only time I forgot me wisdom tooth was tryin' to kill me.

It was worse than bad.

And whenever Louise came round the house, she'd have a go
at me as well. (*BC*) 'Daddy you've *got* to go to the dentist.
You're in so much sodding pain all the sodding time. Please
make a sodding appointment!'

So I sodding did.

I booked at the community dental surgery in Great Bridge –
it's NHS, in one of them rough strip malls. It's at least four
floors. I dunno why, most of the shops in there are either
closed or about to be.

I have to walk up some stairs, past the massage parlour, the
slimming clinic, the acupuncture studio, and this new sex
shop for men – Dan Summers –

And when I reach my floor, I open the door to the dentist's,
finally, I step up to the reception desk – and there's this
woman . . .

Music plays: 'Three Times a Lady' by The Commodores.

She's Caribbean, I know because there's a little Jamaican flag
on the desk. Her hair's in three thick braids, she's got this
incredibly open, kind face – and as soon as she opens her
mouth, I know she's from Dudley.

I tell her I've got an appointment and a right royal pain in
my gob and she says:

(*Dudley*) 'You're lucky, I know someone who can sort that
out for you.' And she smiles at me.

Dr Bhaskar calls me in. I get in the chair and he's using an
entire toolkit to sort me out. He injects me gums with
enough anaesthetic to stun a bull elephant. He starts drilling
and soon there's blood and shards of tooth flying up and
spattering the ceiling.

He's kneeling on my chest for more leverage.

I'm getting more Jamaican the harder he leans in – (*JA*) 'Ah
wha de backside! Rah! Yu wan' kill me?'

The only thing that takes me mind off the whole process is
looking out the door and seeing the receptionist pottering
about, chatting and smiling with the patients. She's glowing–
like Wonder Woman after six Ready Breks.

And I realised – as soon as Dr Bhaskar finished the operation – I knew that all I wanted to do was go back out there – and see her. The receptionist from Dudley.

I get out there and stand at reception, waiting for her to notice I'm there. I read her name tag – it says 'Vilma'.

Finally she sees me and waits for me to say something; so I go:

'Excuse me Miss Vilma – You mus' be a good teef because yu already teef my heart.'

Only trouble is, I'm still numb from the anaesthetic – so all that jus' sounded like:

'Efcufe me Miff Vilma? Yu mft be a thood teef . . .'

She looks at me like I'm a half eediat and writes out the appointment card, gives it to me.

A week later, I'm back for a check-up with Dr Bhaskar – there's been a bit of bleeding from the stitches but nothing fatal. I'm on the mend.

On the way out, I left a thank-you poem for Vilma – it said . . .

'Dear Vilma
To tell you the tooth and to make a start
Since we first parted, I've a cavity in my heart
So I'll stick to my gums and give tongue to my feeling
I'd like to gingivite you for a coffee – is that appealing?
Your sunlight shines from skies above –
Shall you and I sail down the root canal of love?'

I signed with my contact details.

By teatime she's replied via text:

'Mr Henderson, tho your wisdom tooth has now departed
If *you* were to leave, I'd be broken-hearted
So August, if I *May*, please *March* and make a date
I wonder if true speech will help our hearts relate
Here are my details – let's meet and have fun

I like your face and all your teeth – but not the rotten one.
Yours Vilma Clarke.
Smiley emoji, brown clenched fist. Brown thumbs up.'

Oh my God! She accepted my gingivitation. We were going on a date!

This was about eighteen months after Clarice had passed away – it felt like a lifetime of grieving and me beating the crap out of myself every day – everybody around me was saying: 'August, enough.' 'Dad, enough!'

Everybody was right. It was time for the mourning to finish and done – I know you can't really put a deadline on when to stop grieving – but this was a sign.

We met for coffee and cake at Rivington's caff up town, they do the pork baps and the extra-strong tea, it's near the pictures, by the police station with the boarded-up windows.

We had such a lovely time just chatting and getting to know each other. She was so easy to talk to – like having a cup of tea with three Valium on the side.

(*JA*) I told her every. Last. Ting!

About Mama and Papa – about school. The kids – how they've all turned out – Clarice.

Pause.

I even told her about Roisin – and how Clarice died and what that was like for everyone. I cried. On the first date – who does that?

Vilma just held my hand and said she was *sorry for my loss*.

I thanked her.

I asked her if I could see her again – she said yes.

We talked a lot on the phone – it was exciting. We texted a lot during the day.

Courtship by text – it was so romantic.

Happy-face emoji – that just means, y'know, 'I'm happy'.

Wacky-eyes emoji with tongue out means 'I'm crazy about you'.

Brown clenched face is 'I can't wait to see you again'.

I sent her turd with soulful eyes once – by mistake, but I don't think she noticed.

She never replied anyway.

But it didn't matter – we were falling for each other – we went everywhere, we took walks by the canal in Birmingham. We went to Mad O'Rourke's pie factory in Tipton, and Dudley Zoo. How could she not love me after that?

I took her to a Big People's Dance. (JA) 'Old-time tunes for the young at heart.' Vilma can really dance – you wanna see her do the butterfly.

He does the butterfly badly.

(JA) She mek me sweat to backside.

And everyone wanted to meet her . . . we had dinner with Louise and her family and when we got to dessert – Vilma thanked her for looking after me since Clarice died. Louise burst into tears – I had to go outside for some fresh air.

When I came back everybody was crying.

The waiter thought it was the food and gave us a discount, so it all worked out.

We went to see Georgie play football – he's at Redditch now semi-pro and he was brilliant. He can do all the textbook moves –

He's excellent at the 'Jersey Pull'.

He acts it out.

His 'Appeal to Short-sighted Referee' is excellent.

He acts it out.

And his 'Tripped in the Penalty Area by a Complete Bastard' is second to none.

He acts it out.

Vilma talked about marriage a lot – she wanted us to make a formal commitment and after a while, I found myself agreein' with her.

She looked at me in bed the one morning and said: (*Dudley*) 'August? All these problems you've been strugglin' with? They're all in the past – and if we face up to them together – deal with 'em in the here and now – we can build a positive future.'

And then we made love for the third time.

That was a mornin' to remember. I never even knew that kinda thing was possible at our age.

Must be all the hard food.

I loved her idea of *using the present to build a future* – it's quite poetic.

So I'm happy and getting happier. But there's work to be done if you'm getting married nowadays.

I had to apply for the marriage licence and there's a load of documents that need sorting: details of the venue, birth certificate, proof of address and gas or electric bill from the last three months.

So we send off all this stuff. Louise does it all – cos my brain turns to callaloo when I look at documents and complicated official papers and stuff.

She sends it all off. And her and Vilma get into organising the wedding!

This is when the first letter arrive.

It says: 'From the information available it would appear that you are not a British National.

'As you were born in Jamaica you appear to be a citizen of that country.'

Pause.

I give it to Louise straight away, and she says it must be a mistake. She says she'll get back to them and straighten it all out.

Pause.

I gotta straighten summat else out.

Vilma says we shouldn't get married without all of my children there.

She wants to meet Lawrence. He hasn't spoken to me since the funeral. Won't even text me back. So we get Georgie to ask him and hear dis: *(JA)* Lawrence tell him he'll 'consent to a sitdown'.

'Consent to a sitdown?' Like we'm on *The Sopranos* or something? We gonna whack somebody or summat? He's got a bloody nerve.

We went for an Indian at the Momtaj near the Asda – and the minute we sit down, Lawrence starts drinking. He visits the toilet after he's hoovered up an onion bhaji, four pappadums and two parathas and downed four pints of lager.

(Dudley) 'Dutch courage,' Vilma says . . .

I says, 'Dutch? The boy drinkin' for the entire Netherlands, to backside!'

Anyroad, he comes back – she buys him a coffee, asks him why he ent spoken to me for so long.

And then . . . he kinda crumples . . . and tells her everything about what happened that night he took Clarice to inna de back room.

He talks like his mum . . . deep . . .

(*BC, deep*) 'I drove as carefully as I could cos mum was in the passenger seat. I tried to make every stop and start smooth – cos I didn't want her to bounce around so much.

'Mum smelt of cocoa butter and Colgate toothpaste – it was a good smell.

'I liked that she'd made an effort. Even though she was poorly, she wanted to look nice. She'd even put on lipstick.'

Pause.

'When I helped her out the car, I was shocked . . . she'd lost so much . . . so much weight. When I held her arm to help her in, I could feel the bones in her elbow moving.

'Then when I saw Mum's face . . . how she looked at you and that woman – dancing . . . that was the biggest shock of all.

'I hated you then, Dad . . . I really hated you.'

He was shaking and crying when he'd finished. Vilma held his hand *and* mine – and said:

(*Dudley*) 'Alright. It's alright, Lawrence. Look: what happened was wrong. Your dad was an idiot. But we can move forward from this. Let's just keep talking.'

Lawrence looked at me for the briefest of moments and then glanced at his feet.

And I couldn't help thinking of *me* as an eight-year-old, seeing *my* dad in that room in Peckham, with *that other* redhead.

I didn't know what to say.

In the end, he just shook his head, got up, paid the bill and left.

Never even said goodbye or nothin'.

Vilma looked at me.

Later that night, I got a text from Lawrence. It was an emoji. A single brown thumbs up. I guess it's progress.

*Quite a lot of small-/medium-sized envelopes fall from
above – like confetti.*
   He looks up.
   *Then somehow sweeps them all up and puts them with
the others.*
   He sighs.

TEN

Time scooting now.

Tings getting exciting.

Most of the time I'm stayin' at Vilma's. She lives in a
bungalow by Hilltop Road. It's posh up there, they get out
the bath to go for a wee.

Her house is lovely – she's got a dining room, it's all white
furniture – if you spill gravy you'm buggered.

There's an open-plan living area – she's got this chair where
y'lie down, press a button and a foot rest shoots out – like
you're a Black Country Louis XIV.

She's got a sister in Montreal who she's visited a few times
and a brother in Kidderminster who she never sees cos it's
too far.

There's no photos of any ex-boyfriends. She says she burnt
them the day she met me. I reckon she's got 'em in a shoebox
under the bed.

Nah – she's looking after me – I like it an' all . . .

So I'm there most of the time now . . .

But these days – every time I get back to my place – there's
more of them brown envelopes from 'CAPITA'. Horrible
word, 'Capita'. If it's not a venereal disease, it should be.

The letters are confusing. Like they were written by a Dalek.

Every time Louise answers one, they come back with more hoops to jump through.

'We regret long residence in the United Kingdom alone does not confer British nationality.'

Now they want proof of my UK citizenship! They want all this documentation for every year I've been living here. Every year. Don't they understand?

(*JA*) I'm Jamaican! We don't like paperwork and double talk; that's how they get us on the slave ships in the first place.

He goes to the cupboard, a drawer, by the door – and retrieves handfuls of letters.

Louise comes down the shop of an evening to go through all the paperwork with me.

But there's a few years missing – who has fifty-two years of documentation? Do you?

Whatever happens, I've got to sort all this out. Otherwise I'll have to tell Vilma the wedding's off.

Thing is, I don't *want* her to know *any* of this cos if she found out ANYTHIN' was threatening our marriage, it'd mean WAR.

He sings the first few lines of 'War' by Edwin Starr.

But Louise is determined – she's not just *ten*acious she's *eleven*acious!

She keeps saying – (*BC*) 'We'll find all this stuff, Dad; we just need to be methodical.' And she stores everything we've found so far in the shed – I don't want Iqbal worrying about my problems.

Vilma's getting excited about all the preparations. She walks round her kitchen cackling like Hannibal from *The A-Team*: 'I love it when a plan comes together!'

The reception's gonna be at The Back Room. Vilma says I've gotta buy a Marks and Spencer suit. Georgie's trying to get me to buy a red sequinned outfit and pimp it. I think I'll just go for a dark blue single-breasted.

We're talking again – me and Lawrence. It's good. Especially since he started attending the AA meetings.

I'm scared though.

I've had one an' two phone calls from Capita, I keep telling them they've made a mistake, that Louise is sorting it. Eventually I stop answering the phone.

Talk about *pissing on me cornflakes* – where does that expression come from? Somebody must've done it once. You wouldn't do it twice would you?

And now – Vilma's asking me all the time –

(*Dudley*) 'August – why haven't we got an official date yet? People get married every day, why is it taking so long to organise our wedding?'

I do my best to put her off the scent –

(*JA*) 'Oh – we have to be patient, sweetie: everyting take a long time wid these H'Inglish people . . . Look how long it take for them to win the World Cup? Four hundred years.

'We could be a while at this rate.'

She laughs. Calms down a bit.

Then after even more delays, I came up with this brilliant idea.

'Darlin', why don't we have an engagement party to kind of . . . whet everybody's whistle? You don't need no serf-e-ticket for an engagement party. We just need The Back Room, some food and drink and boom! Bob Marley's your uncle.'

That works for a while. We're preparing for the party . . . I was daring myself to be happy . . . everyone's getting on.

I'm seeing more of Lawrence now – we laughed the other day. He told me for the main wedding vehicle he was looking into hiring a Sherman tank . . . damn fool.

He make me laugh though.

Rakim and Louise have been bringing the kids round and making us all exercise to get in shape for the engagement party. I've never done high-intensity training before. I never knew yu could sweat through your eyeballs! Every part of me was worn out.

And Georgie? This was something else: you know that moment when your youngest son takes you out to the Caribbean Cuisine Kart for two patties and a ginger beer? And then he introduces you properly to his boyfriend?

He's called Alex, supports West Brom and he loves Georgie like cook food.

He told me this after the second pattie. (*JA*) Georgie laugh so hard he squirt ginger beer out his left nostril.

They're happy together. I'm happy *for* them.

I made Alex promise to look after him whatever happens. He looked at me and say:

'I've got this, Grandad.'

Cheeky lickle wretch.

But then it all turn to shit.

Time racing now.

I come home one day and find another letter from Capita and there's red writing on this one – that's never good is it?

I'm not even sure I understood what they were going on about:

(*Reads*) 'We are unable to provide you with confirmation that you meet all the requirements for naturalisation.'

52

They're sayin' I might have to leave the country – I don't have 'leave to remain'.

I don't understand. I've been here fifty-two years!

The letter spooked me – so I called Louise – and now she's spooked. More than she was before. She says: (*BC*) 'I'll call them, Daddy. I think we're nearly ready. We've just got a few more documents to find . . . We'll be okay.'

But I can hear a wobble in her voice – it's a little wobble but it's a wobble all the same.

I don't think, 'We're gonna be okay.' It's like watching Mr Blobby on *Dancing on Ice* – I'm thinkin', 'This is a disaster just waitin' to happen.'

Louise calls me back about ten minutes after I've hung up – she says: (*BC*) 'Dad, I've thought about it. You've got to tell Vilma what's going on right away.'

I say, 'Louise – it's just a lickle complication. Let's not bother her wid this foolishness.'

And she yells down the phone:

(*BC*) 'Dad! You're not helping! You've left it all to me – I'm not a lawyer. I'm doing my best – this is a serious situation! They're talking about sending you back to yard!

'You've *got* to tell Vilma – she's going to be your wife!'

She's right.

So I call Vilma and ask her to come round to the house.

When she arrive? I tell her everything.

And Vilma jus' bruk out:

(*Dudley*) 'August? Yu lose yu mind? What part of "a problem shared is a problem halved" do you not understand, to backside? Home Office wan' dash yu 'pon plane an' send yu back to Jamaica – an' it don't enter fe yu head to even pass me a note at bedtime? Wha wrong wid yu?'

I congratulated her on her patois first, obviously – but she didn't laugh. This was serious. She was spooked too. I say:

(*JA*) 'Vilma I feel so shame mi couldn't tell yu nutten. I never know what to do. They keep sayin' I'm illegal. Like *I'm* the crime.'

Yu see me? Me is a big man y'know? An' I was bawling even though I never do nutten wrong.

Vilma grabs me and holds me tight. Says:

(*Dudley*) 'No more secrets alright? We share every problem and we solve them together. From now on, any hint of trouble about *anything* – we tell each other.'

I says – 'Alright Vilma. From now on. I'll tell you everything.'

So blaps. It's a couple weeks later.

It's the night before the engagement party.

Vilma want us to spend the night apart so she can surprise me in the morning. We not getting married yet – what's the big surprise?

We been sleepin' together for months. Trust me – all surprise done.

I practically live with her as it is.

It's pure foolishness – but I agree to it anyway . . . just to make her happy. And when I get back to my yard? There's another letter from Capita – gonorrhoea's wingman:

'Dear Mr Henderson,

'RE: YOUR LIABILITY TO REMOVAL FROM THE UK . . .

'THIS IS TO INFORM YOU – IN ORDER TO ENABLE YOU TO MAKE ARRANGEMENTS TO BE MET OR FOR ONWARD TRAVEL TO JAMAICA.'

Then they add in bold writing: 'Your submissions have been unsuccessful. You must leave the United Kingdom now. If you do not voluntarily leave and removal action is required, you may be subject to a re-entry ban of up to ten years.'

Louise has been answering each letter diligently – this is the response.

'You must leave the United Kingdom now.'

Loud heartbeats.
Heartbeat stops.

A hundred alarm clocks going off in me ears.

The sound of an alarm clock morphs into a phone ringing.

It's Iqbal:

Scratchy phone effects plus the sound of various fireworks going off.

'August I know it's late, but I've had a proper nightmare here.'

Whizz.

'I was having a ciggie at the back of the shop –'

Whizz! Pop! Bang!

'– and when I finished, I chucked it behind me –'

Whizz! Pop! Bang! Whoosh!!

'– and it went through the broken window and, and into the shed.'

Voop! Voop! Vooop! VOOOOOOOOOOOP!!

'Anyway, the cig landed near the fireworks –'

CLIMACTIC – HISS! FIZZ! ZOOM! ZAP! FLASH! BOOM!

'And that means you can't have the engagement party here tomorrow unless you want *to toast the bride for real.*'

Weak farty pop and final fizz . . .
Click brrrrr.

I called Vilma and told her what had happened.

Then she screams in my ear.

Then she calms down and says I should call everyone on my side and say there's been a venue change. We'll have it at my house.

I ring everybody. Then I clean the house from top to bottom. I imagine I'm Vilma and then vacuum like crazy. I'm tired.

Pause.

If the shed's burnt down completely like Iqbal said, that means *all the paperwork's gone.*

All my documents were in a plastic container in the shed. That's where Louise put 'em for safety. Fifty years of bills, newspaper clippings, birth certificates, my mum's passport, pictures of Clarice! Gone!

He screams.
Pause.

I feel sick.

Blackness reach.

Next morning I wake up, shower, shave, and get ready for the engagement party.

But I'm still worried.

What about if the wedding day never happen? What if I have to move to Jamaica? What about me and Vilma?

I put on one and two tunes to relax up meself – Janet Kay: 'Silly Games'.

He sings a bit of the chorus.

Janet voice so high, there's dogs in Aberdeen winin' up their hips . . .

I'm feelin' better – makin' myself laugh and everyting – people start to arrive.

I look out the front door and there's a double-decker bus parked on the pavement outside. Lawrence is here somewhere then.

Then here's Georgie. He fixes my tie. Then points me in the direction of his boyfriend and says: 'Dad – he wants to *wish his future father-in-law* good luck.'

I look at Alex – and he holds up a West Brom scarf – and I'm like: 'Welcome to the family, son! Ah yu dat!'

Georgie just laughs, tells me to stand up straight and mingle wid the guests.

And I can't see Vilma – I'm guessing she's outside, telling people where to put coats. Askin' 'em to hoover when they've got a minute – maybe unblock the drains.

I go outside to look for her and as soon as I'm there – I see Vilma and Louise talking to two blokes.

There's a van blocking the garden gate – the van's got two words written on the side – says:

'IMMIGRATION ENFORCEMENT'.

Rakim comes out – sees these two geezers in uniform shouting at Vilma and his missus.

I tell Rakim, 'Go back in the house!'

Everyting kick off then . . . Time bruk the speed a sound.

One of dem grab me.

Vilma kicks him.

His partner raise him fist to Vilma.

Rakim headbutts him in the chest.

The other one run towards me, grab me and wrestles me to the ground.

I headbutt him in the ear.

Rakim kicks him in the crotch.

Louise is bawlin': (*BC*) 'Rakim, no! They'll send you back to jail!'

That's when Lawrence drives the bus towards all of us and beeps the horn.

I get up, raise me hand to tell him to stop and he runs me over!

Vilma's screamin'.

Rakim's yellin at the top of his voice! (*BC*) 'They don't want us here! They never wanted us here! This is fuckery! Pure and simple racist FUCKERY!!!!'

Pause.

. . . and that's how I got to be here . . . in custody.

ELEVEN

I've never been in an immigration centre before. This one's called 'Brook House Immigration Removal Centre' – it's just behind Gatwick Airport.

I bin here a while now and I wanna go home. I'm tired of eating cheesy beans. All my clothes smell like they were made by Heinz.

Time stop. I don't feel so good. I'm not talking to anybody. I don't want to talk to them. My mind is a mess. I just stay in this room.

The Home Office send me a message through my case worker –

(*Reads*) I will depart *tomorrow* on flight number BA2263 to Kingston Jamaica . . .

I keep sayin':

I have been there since I was eight years old . . .

If only you would just LISTEN:

I came here on my mama's passport.

WHY WON'T YOU BELIEVE ME?

I AM A BRITISH CITIZEN.

I CAN'T JUST GO TO JAMAICA – EVERYBODY I KNOW AND LOVE IS HERE.

WHY CAN'T YOU SEE ME?

Pause.
A shift in point-of-view and position. August begins to hallucinate.

Louise, you see me, don't you? You've always seen me.

I love you – I don't say that enough.

Another shift in point-of-view and position.

Lawrence, you've seen me at my worst. But I'm proud of you.

I'll do right by you I swear.

Looks elsewhere.

Georgie, I see you too. You're perfect. Your mum loved you and now so does Vilma. I beg you take care of her whatever happens to me.

He moves his gaze once more – another shift.

(*To CCTV camera/audience*) Vilma – when we meet I was lost but you find me.

You took my problems and fix them one by one.

I know time is running out.

But my love for you is constant, never-ending.

And I *will* marry you, Vilma.

I don't care how long it takes or what I have to do.

I want to marry you. So mi soon come.

As August says this last bit, the rest of the set disappears from around him – it's as if the Home Office have decided the show must not go on.

Cross-fade from complete blackout to video as:
We hear sounds of a a jumbo jet taking off loudly and fading into the distance.

August disappears during blackout.

Hostile environment/testimony clips:
1. An opportunity to play in audio/archive news footage of a politician explaining the hostile environment.
2. First-person testimony by a male Windrush scandal survior.
3. Second bit of archive/news footage – perhaps someone from the Home Office, doubling down on reducing immigrant figures.
4. Personal testimony by a female Windrush scandal survivor.
5. More news/audio clips.
6. Third testimony from a Windrush scandal victim.
7. Yet another government gobblededook statement.

Visual effects here:
The screen melts – then fills with the faces of the Windrush detainees – from Anthony Bryan to Paulette Wilson, Kenneth Williams, Junior Green, Junior Griffiths, Jeffrey Miller, Briggs Levi Maynard, Winston Jones, Sarah O'Connor, Hubert Howard, Richard Wes Stewart and more – they fill up the screen.

And then there's a black-and-white photograph of August in 1962 – with his mum.

Complete blackout.

Ends.